The Fall

The Rules of Paradise
Leaving Xaia
Voices over Water
Staggered Lights
Shadow Wars
Isolation in Action

The Fall

D. Nurkse

Alfred A. Knopf   *New York   2004*

THIS IS A BORZOI BOOK
PUBLISHED BY ALFRED A. KNOPF

Copyright © 2002 by D. Nurkse

www.randomhouse.com/knopf/poetry

Knopf, Borzoi Books, and the colophon are registered trademarks of
Random House, Inc.

Owing to limitations of space, all acknowledgments for permission to print
previously published material may be found at the end of the book.

Library of Congress Cataloging-in-Publication Data
Nurkse, D., 1949–
The fall : poems / by D. Nurkse.
p. cm.
ISBN 0-375-70976-2 (pbk)
I. Title.
PS3564.U76 F35 2002
811'.54—dc21
2002022341

Manufactured in the United States of America
Published, September 29, 2002
First Paperback Edition, April 15, 2004

To Beth, with love

Contents

I I I

Prologue

The Threshold

As I waited for the doctor
I realized nothing was wrong with me,
just a voice whispering the word
triage, a few sleepless nights,
a change in the weather, great winds
visible in the crests of trees
I could glimpse through a vent
at the far end of the corridor,
the immense power of dreams
unchecked by waking. . . .

And I prepared to apologize
for presuming on his time—perhaps
the apology itself would waste
a minute marked for a real patient—
but he arrived from nowhere,
took my hand, and spoke
calmly, consolingly, as to a child,
yes, yes, he'd seen the tests,
in fact he had them on his person,
somewhere in his calfskin briefcase—

and I watched his lips, avid for a pause,
so I could whisper: *it's all a mistake.*

I

Sunlight

I trained a magnifying glass
on the ant with the crumb
and he stepped away
from the pool of light.
I held the beam
wherever he was going.
At once he shriveled
to a tiny black line
whose ends rose slowly
to meet each other.
I aimed at my hand
and sensed that fire
infinitely distant, close,
then inside me:
when I dropped the lens
I felt no comfort
and called my father's name.

Treasures of the Cove

A tiny dromedary, a doorknob,
a bust of Trajan, eyes sealed with mica,
a red egg, a whorled brain . . .

Each pebble glinted
with the sea's life.

Amazing, my father said,
but he kept his eyes on Drummond Rock.

If I had dared
I would have shown him
my empty hand and let him murmur
how beautiful.

He had a week to live
and on a spit of land
a white collie was chasing
something I couldn't make out—
a fly? a frisbee?—
so free and enraptured
by what eluded it.

A funnel dipped under the skyline
but its smoke-wisp remained.
That's the ferry, my father said,
late for Matinicus Island.

His strides were colossal.
I ran in his shadow
but gingerly, so the shells

in my pocket wouldn't shatter:
whelks, spiral staircases
into nothing, mother-of-pearl shards
like broken sunsets, a clamshell
found an hour ago, now dry, gray,
useless except to hear
my own ocean.

Northbound

A bell tolled six times
on an island in the fog
and my father turned toward it.

Angelus or a signal?
Where the reefs must be,
a buoy chimed at random.

How to row toward a voice
once it has fallen silent?
He listened tight-lipped:

bitterns, gagging laughter,
slap and hiss of Castine,
creaking oars, my crying.

A white hand cupped us
so we faced each other
entirely inside the mind.

Then he began stroking powerfully,
a vein swelled on his forehead,
his blue knuckles rose like pistons,

even I could sense us circle
under the spell of his right arm,
and he lost himself counting

in his exile's language—
twenty, a thousand, as if our home
lay beyond those enormous numbers.

The Play Hour

1 THE SANDBOX

We held a funeral
for a dead ladybug
and smoothed the earth
with the belly of a spoon.

Who'd count the tiny dots
now, or study the long crawl
and sudden flight?

We dug a pit
for a hemlock leaf
curled into itself.

We said last rites
for a fleck of mica—
who'd watch it flash
at evening, as if to hint
at a powerful secret?

We buried our hands
up to the wrist.
The dark no one sees
bit under our nails.

We wouldn't wait long:

the sparrow arrived
just out of reach
to hold us safe
in a bright indifferent eye.

2 THE SWING

When we soared
we longed to plummet.

We rose toward sunset
side by side, Converse Hi Tops
aimed at red Antares.

Father pushed
and puffed on his pipe,
nearer, more remote,
as the yard assembled itself,
delicate with distance:

dusk dog, twilight cat,
dazzling kitchen window
where Mother peeled a carrot
and stared at shadows.

Why were we so lonely?
At last we felt no one
behind us and slowly
returned amazed to earth.

3 THE SEESAW

Perfectly equal
we wait for crazy laughter
to lift one and let the other
run sobbing from the game.

Initials

We'd been drawing in chalk,
surprised they would allow us
to sign the world.

We made the grid for a game,
a ladder to paradise.

I wrote her name.
She entered mine.
I inscribed a heart, she the date.

We'd been given everything:

the little dusty box,
the road stretching
all the way to the neighbor's house,

the threshold, the invisible watcher,
the huge hour until sunset.

First Date

She admired my collection
of cracked robins' eggs,
even touching one,
and glanced at my watch.

I pointed out the praying mantis
enchanted in death, the tiny shadow
he cast in his matchbox.

I let her hold the penknife
only a man could open.

I unwrapped the bottle cap.
I was too modest to mention
the fight I won it in.

I dusted off the little mouse,
its paws drawn to its chest
in disbelief.
All the fur still clung to it.

It was evening.
The lawn sprinklers clicked on.

The breeze in the crawl space
turned dark and wet.
Her mother called her name.

She thanked me
and turned a different profile,
kissing me once
hard on the forehead,
one leg thrown back for balance,

then leaving with that dancer's step,
pausing sometimes
to wave at the night between us.

Red-and-Silver Schwinn

I would never learn.
She would never love me.

When I wriggled on that cruel seat
a blind force—perhaps hope—
smashed me into the sprinkler system.

Even when I wheeled it,
the bike jackknifed.

It seemed the fall
was planned within me.

Polite with rage
I refused training wheels.

I carried the frame tenderly
over newly sodded lawns.

Once it was my burden
there was nowhere we could not go.

The Migraine

Coat draped
in the curtain gap,
towel under the door—
in this pitchdark room
I could be a thought
inside my own mind

but my father whispers:
glass of water.
Fresh compress.
No, he is too proud,
he just lies like a magnet
where the darkness begins

and I walk toward him
memorizing the traps
—slippers, Sunday paper—
with the cup in my hand
trying not to breathe

always stopping dead
an inch from the wall
that glides ahead of me:
now I am at his right hand

but if I speak his name
or the word *Father*
he will suffer, so I wait,
call me, I am here,
I am right beside you
though you cannot know.

The Dog

At twilight we walk each other
in the snowy park.
The leash yanks us apart.
Our trails mix crazily.
Haven't we always traveled
in a series of lunges
away from a missing center?
Something we can't name
obsesses us at the plinth
of the frozen birdbath,
and again under the belly
of Sherman's bronze horse.
Is there a secret passage
to squeeze through and be free
of the endless command?
We shout *heel*, our voice
slurs with longing, at last
we'll enter our own lit door
and there undo our studded collar,
mete out stale friskies, comb
matted hair, turn three times
on nothing, and whimper
in a dream whose ending
everyone knows but us.

Pennies for Flies

With a whisk and notepad
to tally what I killed
I prowled my father's study.
I listened for wings.
I practiced swatting,
scared of my fierce grace.
The first one I hit
still seemed make-believe.
Many I found dead in the webs
like things waiting to be born.
Unless they were transparent
I blew their clinging threads away
and saved them in my matchbox.
Others in the lamp bowl were dead
but perfect, and I had to flatten them
slightly, or remove a leg.
At last they were a number: nine:
one was missing and I paced
waiting for him to land.
Everywhere he was a stain,
a blemish, a buckling seam,
a bud in the bed of roses
that circled the wall forever.
Then night invited a companion
to watch me from the window,
an old man, remarkably small,
his right hand raised and in his eyes
that look of amazing patience.

Left Field

Told I threw *like a girl*
I waited out in the shadows

while the infielders made spectacular leaps
—by luck or memory of the future?

Some threw like older girls,
some hurled streaks of evening,

all grew equally remote
as night fell and the voices
singing *no batter, no pitcher*
faded under crickets.

I pounded my glove,
spat, dug my cleats
savagely in the sod
and growled *swing*.

Secretly, I was proudest of my skill
at standing alone in darkness.

The Rules of the Game

A sticky thread between my fingers.

God knows what happened.

I'd been dreaming of baseball—

Dodgers vs. Giants
at Ebbets Field, Snider at bat
hitting .379, a 1-2 fastball
about to nick the inside corner—

then this spasm
and all my pennants
hung slightly crooked.

A breeze blew inside me.
It no longer mattered
if the drive cleared the fence.

Mystery. I asked my mother:

and she sighed and began searching
in the highest shelf of the bookcase.

The Hellmann's Jar

Lucky sealed in a tarantula and a praying mantis.
He had reamed airholes in the lid.

He invited me.
These are the Gods of War.

The bug eyes ignored each other.
That too, Lucky explained, was deep combat.

We stared and waited.
Sometimes we glanced furtively
at the kitchen clock.

The fighters stood enchanted,
camped in bodies that seemed immense,
gossamer legs arcing
with the contour of the glass.

Later, the question:
how to give them food and drink
without disturbing the trance of strategy?

Lucky blew in atomizer mist.
They would eat each other.

On the third day we woke.
The spider was still alive
immobile in its corner.

The praying mantis had vanished.

A good soldier, Lucky said.
He gave his life.

Darkness

I closed my eyes and swung.
When I opened them
the ball was clearing the fence.

I shut my eyes and threw.
The famous cleanup batter
trudged back to the dugout
kicking his helmet before him.

Darkness.

I kissed my friend
and felt her tongue
talkative in my mouth
promising gifts
I wouldn't dream of.
I didn't dare look.

For a moment
I held the night sky
in all its frailty.

I walked home alone.

Sentinel lamps
shone of their own accord
in houses where parents
moaned in love or dreams.

The world was composed
of leftover trees
and fireflies from before.

I was less than the breeze.

Still the massive door
swung open at my touch.

Born Again

My father asked me wearily
not to leave the dental floss
looped around the faucet.
I prayed for him then;
not just forgiveness
but the Balm of Gilead.
Let Christ heal him,
reveal his grave errors,
show him the Way
to love me and be free . . .

As I knelt for hours
facing my blank wall
I came to admire a pinprick,
a bristle suspended
in dry paste,
a wallpaper seam
miraculously crooked—

never before had I seen
this world this close.

Paradise

Lucky prized open the capsules.

Feverfew, phenobarb,
rosehip, sharkskin,
methamphetamine.

He sifted the powder
on a Polaroid negative.

He weighed the dose
on his mom's scale.

It didn't register,
though that needle trembled
at breath itself.

He gulped.

He looked at me
with bright eyes.

This world was silent
like a clock between ticks.

I was so happy
he hadn't offered.

But did he know
how far I'd traveled

from the immaculate family room—
catalogs on low tables,
white shag carpet—

how old I'd grown
just by watching?

Jumping Off the Fire Tower for Laura

1

I fell and loved falling.
I practiced suffering.
I lived in midair,
in my own breath,
in the womb of flight,
a passerby.

For a moment
I had power
to make her know me.

I passed a spiraling seed,
moths like ashes,
a dragonfly, maniacally level.

I was free. I could choose
whatever ending I wanted
so long as it was a shattering blow.

2

I lay in triumph
swathed in bandages
with little tin clasps
while the clock ticked.

A mouse was eating the house,
spitting out the sad parts.

The water in my glass
grew less and less cloudy.

In another room
the doctor bargained
in his prissy voice.

In another year
he'll be himself again.

Bread and Wine

1

I mixed Wheaties,
Nesquik, yeast, and condensed milk,
baked it, froze it, fried it,
basted it with Miracle Whip.

When the loaf had risen
I broke it for my parents.

I was amazed. They ate it
with only mild tics,
my mother with level eyes,
my father with a quivering Adam's apple,
each in the sadness of deep love.

I had nourished them
and I still couldn't whistle
or name the hours.

When it was finished
I saved the crumbs
in SaranWrap, for the next Sabbath.

2

I sipped from each glass
when the guests were gone
and felt myself
the center of fierce devotion.

The living room embarked
on a circular journey,
the ashtray changed places
with the Ping-Pong trophy.

Desperate, I nibbled saltines.

When my mother stopped and stared
I signaled to her
in a panic that seemed someone else's.

A great happiness, that no one can feel,
had come between us.

At the Stage of Riddles

I tiptoed behind my father
and cupped my hands
over his eyes and whispered:
    Guess Who?

Always he thought hard
and answered gravely:
Eisenhower. Or *DiMaggio.*

And I was happy, knowing
he was safe from my love.

Almost I envied him
the brevity of his confinement
in the unknowable darkness.

Under the Porch

Lucky peeled the wings
from a fly
and gave them to me,
as Father once trusted me
with the tiny screws
when he fixed his glasses.
But in my cupped hands
they disappeared.
It was a miracle.
We looked everywhere.
The fly buzzed—
how could it still buzz?—
much louder than before.
At last we reconciled ourselves
and knelt with great compassion
and watched as it moved
in an almost line,
then an almost circle,
there in the crawl space
under the huge brushes
rigid with shellac:
and we were rapt
as if we'd found
the way out of loneliness.

The Fall

1

My father died.
I sat beside my mother
writing notes to the family.

She addressed, I sealed.
The responsibility was mine.
If I licked too long
our names would blur—
too quick and the card
might flutter out

where a stranger could see it.
From that high sofa
I could peek into the garden.
Apple blossoms whirled like snow.

What a long way home.
But we were home.
My thigh prickled against hers.

Dusk, and still a pile left.
Why did we have so many cousins?

I watched her severe white shoulder
for any sign of weakness.

Now it was night, May night,
the petals stopped twirling
in deference to darkness

and we'd left someone out
so important he'd be shocked,
he'd be horrified,

but who?
The uncle in Stockholm?
The niece in Australia?

It was past bedtime, a steeple said so,
and still my mother ruined her eyes
under that weak lamp
inscribing a single name
and names of distant cities.
Prague, Vienna, Tallinn.

A moth thudded softly
against the screen,
demanding to be let out.

2

Now my brother and I
play soccer so gracefully—
before we were sacks of bones,
puppets twitching to desire.

We dribble through each other
like smoke . . . the goal
marked by a shirt and lunch box,
the score a thousand to nothing . . .

We rule this six-foot gap,
just the two of us.
Our father below
stumbles in his grave.

3

Nipple with a little brown circle
around it, and a hair—
I saw this in a mirror,
she dressing, he laid out:
the hair astonished me:
then it vanished
in my white cloud of breath.

4

A child whose father died
is following the body,
limping a little
because he skinned his knee
in the championship game . . .

Something holds him back
but something draws him forward,
rivets him to the amber taillights
of the receding black Dodge.

Sometimes he slips in an extra step
or coaxes himself forward
pumping his arms, but discreetly,
so no one will guess
the blood is hardly caked . . .

And I watch
from the crest of the cedar
where I've been robbing
the songbirds' nests,
bits of shell in my pocket.

Yolk sticks to my shorts
and dries on my thigh.
I cannot speak, the owl might hear,
but I whisper, *hurry*.

As if he hears me
the child stumbles and begins racing
and the gate closes behind him.

The bells start tolling,
first mourning, then gloating.
I count noon, midnight, echoes,
until there are no more numbers
but only music,
and the breeze rocks me.

Cat's-Eye

My father waved good-bye.
I didn't wave back,
scared I might drop
my new cold smoky marble.

At the core a spiral
glinted and coiled
like a small windy flame
turning in on itself.

That night my mother
shook me from a dream,
whispering he was dead,
he was dead, he was dead,
as if to teach a language
and I answered: he is dead.

Even in sleep
my hands had not opened.

II

An Opening in the Largest City

The lovers look perfectly natural
next to these atrocious paintings
of the Sea of Okhotsk and the Sea of Marmara.
I'm the one who needs a prop,
an invitation or just a wineglass.
I've worked all my life on this mask
of fascinated suffering, still a guard
might arrive at any minute and whisper
and I'd have to nod, summoned.

Occasionally a distinguished guest
pauses to peer at a gilt frame
and murmur: *Extraordinary.*

All these seas are dead.
I can see my face reflected
in the terribly thick patina,
and the arc of her cigarette:
the trick is not to focus
on the foreground, the linseed scumble,
the knowing brushstrokes that convey
order, chaos, a misty shore
and the attraction of irresistible winds.

At Payless

The panhandler who knew my name
lies covered with a blue wool blanket,
the doorway where he slept
sealed with a strip of tape
—a barrier a sparrow could pass:

two plainclothes write in notebooks,
each listening to a different radio:

I'll give my quarter instead
to the girl who waits at Payless,
who rocks on her heels in a dream,
only a paper cup placed carefully
outside the ring of frozen urine
to show she's still asking.

Empire Boulevard

I wanted to leave this neighborhood
before dark: now I wait
on the hard sofa in your lobby.
Either you've slept absurdly late
or you never came home . . .
Security watches me and taps
on the pommel of his nightstick.
Framed in the door a hooker
passes with many sideways glances,
then joggers and a Jehovah's Witness.
I haven't slept in two days.
Better to leave now
than to let you see me
with this face of long sickness,
meek with an old man's desire.
I'd hoped to leave this town
before the curfew, the snipers,
especially before the negotiations:
and now Security flosses his teeth
and stares straight at me
as if into a mirror,
his eyes dazzling with evening.

The Engagement

We were coaxing each other to paradise
and also locked in a game of chess
—each cheating to lose.

Among the caresses
there was one we withheld
with great pride and cunning,
and among the names we called,
incandescent with loss,
some were just cries.

Always the cat watched,
switched the tip of her tail,
and licked one paw,
then the other.

On Maze Street, steps receded,
and the cries of children
mimicked each other,
stupid, stupid,
absurdly faint and clear.

The clock ticked scrupulously
as if hoarding a treasure.

Radio music vanished
sad or ecstatic—
all we heard was silence.

We'd come to the world
without us—wrinkled sheet,
bright fading stain,
empty room filling with dawn,
two cloudy wineglasses
touching at base and rim.

Riding West with Laura

Between Utica and Buffalo
the billboards have grown old.

A mother pouring milk
for her son's Wheaties.

A father waving from his blue DeSoto.

You hum like a child beside me.

In the weed-grown Baptist parking lot
a sign announces a wedding:
Jay & The Americans will perform
Great Hits of 1961.

Now it's dusk and the fireflies
kindle and happiness
approaches fast
but swerves at the last second.

Our odometer begins to shine
like an emerald, proclaiming
we've been traveling all our lives.

The little white motels
gleam like sugar cubes
and promise pools and telephones.

The ruby in the gas gauge
says there's nothing left.

Only static on the radio,
news of assassinations,
famine, giant mirrors
hoisted into space.

Laura, it's no lie:
this wheat goes on forever.

Black River

1

We slipped steadily
through the broken forest
toward the heron's silhouette.
When we were close,
almost touching,
it shrugged and launched itself
on wings so huge
they seemed a burden.

We feathered our oars
and let the current carry us.
That water was so calm
we felt we were dead,
our faces slightly blurred
by the breeze, by happiness.

It all happened in reflection:
the dragonflies coupling
in midair, the entrance
to the grove of charred pines,
each taller than the last.

The berry cove, the diving rock
on which there was no foothold.
We lay together in a clearing,
hoping it was not a path.

We were closer
than moss to broken twigs.

All that came between us
was light and shadow.

2

The way home was upstream.
Our hands ached from gripping.
At each inlet we hushed,
hungry for that trance,
eager to be seen and known
again, to be whole, to feel
the wind from that flight.

The Stone House at Black River

1

We didn't use the fly
or the little brown circle
under the wine bottle
(though it was half-erased),
we used the Mind—

as if there were no gap
between death and the word *death*.

2

Always soon and mostly never
the cat tipped over the waffle mix.

3

Because we were alike
as two buttons
we invented this great war
between God and Satan.

4

The last sip of wine,
last blowing curtain,
a strand of copper hair drifting
in the breeze from Cape Rosier—
so much love seemed a bad omen
but the last days grew more beautiful
night by night.

5

If marriage solves sex
what cures marriage?

6

Little door we may open
but only as the breeze.

Honeymoon in Varia

We woke at dawn
envying our shadows
their chance to return.

We were beyond our depth
in happiness.

We had become the same person
but with a mind of her own.

In the next room
two lovers were dressing,
stumbling, quarreling—

to make it easier to part?
The walls were so thin!

Varia: sleepy town
between the wheat and the desert.

Plaza, two swallows, dusty fountain.

Distant mountains
or perhaps just clouds—

and we still sorting our clothes
jumbled on the wicker chair:
yours . . . yours . . . yours . . .

That room was so tiny
everything we touched was us.

Leaving Zaragoza

We slept together
in a dream
but also wide awake.

While we dressed,
a bell rang very faintly
deeper in the city.

We had to stop buttoning
to count; our zippers
drowned out the hour.

Before we left
we searched under the bed
for a ring or a visa—

were we lucky enough
to have lost something
that could never be replaced?

When we closed the door
gingerly, with bated breath,
we remained on the inside,

quarreling and making up,
kissing, telling bad jokes,
there in the empty room

though the key turned
and the steps moaned
under the weight of shadow.

The Formal Gardens at Coimbra

The children behind the rhododendron
threw pebbles at us:
first mica flecks,
then gravel, then stones,
missing deliberately,
by a hair, then not missing.

We the newlyweds
clasped on our bench
scored with strangers' names
looked up blankly,
imperious, aggrieved,
then turned back
rapt to each other.

At last we rose
with great dignity
and walked hand in hand
as slowly as possible,
sometimes pausing to arrange
a strand of the other's hair,

past the topiary shrubs,
the busts of betrayed lovers,
the chain-smoking groundskeeper,
the fountain with its rusty pennies,

into the walled rose garden
where old couples who look alike—
as if sex had borrowed
a little from each—

feed the dusty pigeons
or read each other snippets
from Ecclesiastes, Solomon,
all the songs of ecstatic loss.

Riches of the Interior

At Varia the suicides
are reborn as crows
and camp at the tree line
to warn of fog.

Here in the vineyards
the self-killed are bees,
flying very slowly
into spilt wine.

When you come to the capital
a sparrow will follow you
through the immense plaza
shyly, at arm's length,
only to flinch at your crumb.

Pity these souls
who could not endure
our burden of endless gifts.

Marriage in the Infinite City

We caressed the cat
instead of each other.
We gave the cat
the biscuit we most wanted:

just frittered it away
between thumb and forefinger
and the cat mouthed the crumbs
politely, with glistening gums.

We had a single heart
but it had turned against us.
We would have waited forever
so long as it was for us

and the cat stalked
from sink to hot plate
in that tiny room,
even the crook of its tail
measuring, judging . . .

If we could have had sex
only in bed or made love
just with our bodies . . .

Laundry hung dazzling
in the window, smoke
rose at a cant,
the sun set.

The cat knew us too well
and slept to forget us,
twitched, bared its fangs,
then rolled over,
presenting its belly
to be stroked in a dream.

The Rapture

A blue vein throbs at her temple.
She climbs a glittering Stairmaster
while her ex-husbands wander the snowy streets
writing Kabbalistic signs in chalk
announcing the end of the world or just
the dawn of an age of impenetrable omens.

Sometimes she sips
volcanic water from a vial
or consults the gauges
that show her temperature,
pulse rate, the long wave
of desire cresting to Alpha.

She is higher now than Lhasa,
the Tien Shan, or Everest.
A softly taped votive drum
urges her never to return.

No bigger than fleas, her husbands
parade with placards reading
Repent. The Rapture is Tonight.
If one spots another in the crowd
he kneels to copy that rival slogan
—always room for one more portent—
while the surge of commuters
leaves a gap the shape of the body.

Custody Wars

One seed of chaos had been lost
in the Motar Galaxy.
If it was not found
the infinite stars
would all implode.

The children sat rigid
in pajamas, transfixed
in that constant shifting gleam:
at their feet a heap of dolls,
dinosaurs, skeletons, small gods,
a king with a key in his spine,
a mound of unopened bills,
roach motels, a little wedge
of mouse poison, gnawed at the lid,

and I stood behind them
becoming used to darkness.
The known stars drew back
like a curtain opening
and swiftly we entered
deep space, pure waiting,
each bound by a cold ray,
each with a finger to his lips,

while in another room a phone
pealed—perhaps the final offer—
faint as all the charms of earth.

The Part

Perhaps the barber was my father
or maybe he was God.
Snip, snip: calm voice
possibly from between my ears
offering a choice and no choice;
this is your part; wet or dry?

Three combs on a frayed towel—
one tortoiseshell, one transparent,
one clogged with white hair—
and a bottle of Cutler's bay rum
sealed with a foil wisp.

So many scissors; how could he choose?
So many razors; pearl-handled, quarter moon,
and one long glistening strop
dangling from a high nail.

In the mirror the reverse gold letters
were true again and I watched
snow pelting on Avenue B.

Still I expected rioters,
but the world had taken a turn
toward unimaginable wealth
on every block but this.

A hooker shuffled
in the door to AXIS FLATS,
blowing on her manicure.
A boy in a pink hood

was crying the name of a drug.
I could read his lips:
crystal meth.

And the barber said to me:
you are my long lost son
returned to me from the grave.

No, that was my voice,
his was saying:
a little more off the ears?

He showed me the back of my head.
I approved—could I have returned it?—
and even in that tilting glass
I saw the shudder of snow
incandescent with trapped breath.

There in the street the homeless
were sweeping out their cardboard precincts,
and the man who believes in judgment
was resting, no longer preaching,
just holding out a little fading sign
that read: *I AM THE ONE WHO IS CALLED I AM.*

A Couple in Garden City

1

Great Love, like a hostile parent,
always watched us
to see if our nails were clean,
if there were crumbs
at the corners of our mouths—

imperious Love, irascible,
muttered about a catastrophe
we would never know, close
and remote as a lit window—

you will never know how I suffered
in Logos because of your ignorance

and we lovers unbuttoned shyly
in the night of war and amazing wealth,
sad for each other, telling each other
little jokes to make it easier,
wanting nothing except twilight:

but that Love always with a project:
the darkest night; sharpest pencil;
softest pillow; cruelest betrayal;

so we blessed each other
in a language we invented,
more silent than thought,
each word backlit as in a dream
where there is no choice but kindness,

and that Love, furious, searched
among the laws for a single name,
erased on the day we met.

2

The rake splayed on the lawn,
a hose glittered over daffodils,
the brillo pad circled the dish,
smoke hovered above the chimney,
the comb journeyed with many setbacks
through a forest of scented hair,
and the voice cried in a dark room.
If we were lost in a second of happiness,
how bright will we burn in paradise?

Not even God may enter the past
yet we sneaked there
hand in hand and carved our names
in the pith of the apple tree.

If loneliness were a taxi,
I'd give it our old address:
1 Pison Drive, a block from Euphrates:

picket fence, gambrel roof,
bent hoop, bug light, dangling tire,
in the garage a bike with training wheels,
waiting to take us to our father's mansion.

The Wilson Avenue Kings

A child with glittering eyes
spat on me, slashed my jacket
with his box cutter

and now the cop holding him
in a hammerlock ordered:
hit as hard as you want.

Snow drifted in whorls
in the arc of a high lamp.
A dog's silhouette paced
behind a frosted window.

As I backed away
trying to make each step slower
eyes in hallways
picked up my trembling.

Each door was covered
with one stroke of a letter
of an immense name

and the cop shouted after me:
Faggot. I risked my life.

Saint Peter's Basement

These homeless were screened
for gentleness by the Board
and I may leave them alone
with knives and cooking wine.

My cot marked Volunteer
creaks in an alcove
and the voices before dawn
cry but do not fight,

cry for Zion, for Cotonou,
for a long dream of flight
that opens into Sterifab
and the 6:00 A.M. school bus

to the Remand Center, so huge
its address is a whisper.

Lucky Ford

A woman asked me:
are you Lucky Ford?
That was the year of razor loneliness
and I said, of course I am.
She beamed and asked:
did we meet in Palm Springs?
I nodded: Palm Springs.
Her cheek was taut, waxed.
Behind her, black rain
flickered in a gold-framed mirror.
The reception had broken up:
only the walnut cheese log remained,
stoved-in in the spun-glass chafing dish.
And your wife of twenty years,
she said, who was so gentle?
Divorced, I answered,
gone for no reason,
after a fight I cannot understand.
And the woman bit her lip
and murmured, *I knew you were a stranger.*

The Tower Overlooking the City

I asked: could I become like you
through suffering?
You shook your head.
No.
You looked at your watch.
I wanted to know:
was there a way?
You had no idea.
You leaned forward
and touched my sleeve
with two fingers.
Was this what you had come for,
across that distance
so great nothing could measure it,
not even zero?
I offered you water.
I looked in the freezer
for an ice cube.
I hadn't mentioned food.
Perhaps you were starving?
I heated some broth.
Serenity, I said, serenity—
the chance to think clearly—
the tower that overlooks the city—
you frowned as if my words
contained a threat,
a contradiction to some truth
you had that I did not.

You began your preparations for leaving.
You sprinkled ash on the floor
and wrote your name

and wiped it out.
I reminded you how I'd visited you
in Saint Rose's, bringing flowers,
vitamins, cards, news,
how terrified I'd been
that I might never have the chance
to thank you for the last time—
you smiled wanly.
Your presence here was not permitted.

You apologized and I heard
your quick step in the hall
and the old bitter cough
and I knew you were gone.
The neighbors' argument resumed
behind the paper-thin wall
and the sirens again converged
on an imaginary fixed point
in Flatbush or Central Brooklyn.
I rinsed your cup,
then wished I'd preserved
the pattern of the tea leaves.
Moonlight touched your chair.
For a long time I sat in darkness
remembering the comfort
you had brought to my life.
My clock dial was growing dim—
soon it would be dawn
and the immense searchlights
would slowly become invisible.

A Path in Grace

The keeper in the guardhouse
asked the name of the grave.
He licked his thumb and wheezed,
unfolding a huge map.

I wanted to explain: my hope
was to be lost among monuments,
not to see my father face to face.

But he ran his finger up broad avenues
and down frayed seams, murmuring:
Liberation . . . Grace . . . Ocean View.

I never listened to directions
and least of all to his. I nodded
until his kindness was satisfied.

He asked, when did your father die?
I wanted to say: *forever*
but sensed a trick: *1958.*

He nodded—a gnarled Estonian
my age or my father's—
and turned a wrought-iron key
in the brass-studded lock.

He waved. I waved back.
The door slammed. I heard him shouting
Good luck! through the massive wall.

In the cold I smelled cabbage soup,
fresh black bread, garlic so strong
I had to blink back tears.
Ahead lay the serried graves:

obelisks, ice-sheathed,
bearing the legend *Father*,
small scattered stones
saying *Child*, constant snow
filling corners of letters,
beautifully articulating
the weld of my bootprint,

then erasing my tracks
so that I was lost
as I had prayed to be,
not in limbo or resurrection,
Gethsemane or Elysian Fields.

Once I felt watched
and saw a rabbit peering
solemnly from behind a headstone.
When I knelt it bounded away
looking over its shoulder
with astonished reproachful eyes.
I wiped the grave with my sleeve
and read: *I Love You.*
We Will Never Be Separate.

Two yellow chrysanthemums
had shriveled to globes
of finely whorled dust
in a jug sealed

with a scrim of green ice.
Two massive bolted doors
led into the ground.

As far as I could see
angels hovered, cherubs,
headless victories, snow.

Somewhere, perhaps among the living,
a bell began pealing,
insidious, solemn, obsessive,
and there was no one left to tell
the echo from the final stroke.

III

Music from an Inner Room

I'd been sick many nights
and my sheet clung to me
like a lover's body—so complicated
in its folds and twists—

but my pillow rolled itself
in a tight little ball
like a loyal child
afraid to hurt a parent.

Who filled the glass
just out of reach on the nightstand?

Who cinched the curtain even tighter,
so that I might guess at an enormous city
—steeples and monuments—
in that thread of thin snow light?

Music played in another room,
always the same song
ending or beginning.

Once I heard the cry of someone suffering:
a voice that seemed to listen to itself.

Sometimes the hiss of sleet on shingles,
or bells, very faint.

Perhaps a great festival was at hand
and my long wait was over.

Sometimes a sparrow sang
in a language so difficult
it brought tears to my eyes.
Yet I heard my father's name,
and my mother's, and mine as a child.

What hand brought me grapes
in a little china dish?
Whose voice read to me
whenever I dozed off—

the story of an immense journey,
a fortunate return, winter,
a lover grown old waiting?

The Book of Splendor

1   THE BODY

I found a dead bee
curled in the tiny print.
I breathed on it gently
so it would not cover
the word *Unknowing.*
I didn't want it lost
outside that text
that spoke so lovingly
of two gates—first Mercy,
then Fear—
that lead to the inner world.

2   THE MIND

Detachment, the book says.

If you had detachment
the shock of the fall
would be like words on a page.

Even when you were whole
all you wanted was to heal.
Now study calm.

And I've memorized each page,
the margin stains, the errata,
the foxing, the cunning worm holes,
the colorless thread that holds my place
each night until the last.

The Prognosis

Naked on the examining table
I studied the doctor's certificates
and saw he was astonishingly old.
He had practiced in Narva
before the war, even before the armistice,
he had the blessing of the savants of Tartu,
and behind the letters of his name
an artist had lovingly drawn shadows.

A silhouette hovered in frosted glass,
a shy knock, I myself said *Come in,*
he entered, glistening bald pate,
pronounced stoop, absurd burden
of charts, documents, perhaps maps?
and he began to question me:

Did I really love you?
Did I still want children?
Did I ever want to die?

As he spoke he wrote effortlessly
—or perhaps in one long spasm—
never meeting my eyes, sheet after sheet
darkening with glyphs, while he coughed,
while he framed questions,
long after we finished speaking.

I tried to glimpse my name
or yours, or Domodossola,
in that upside-down scrawl.

In the slanting afternoon silence
I could hear the swish of traffic
forty flights down, a distant jet,
and the sighs of other patients
in the outer corridor,
their small talk, their endless wait,
and I the only barrier
between the aging of the body
and the safety of the page.

At Mary Magdalene

If I make myself still
the voices will pass through me
baffled and feast
on the things of this room
calling the night glass
fool and the light switch
faggot.

Little dusty knickknacks
that I failed to care for
on my journey from home:
postcard from Castine
foxed at one corner,
frayed silk rose
with a rigid serrated leaf,
key, tiny mirror . . .

Tarnished now, eddying
in the whirlpool of judgment:
bad mirror . . . stupid rose . . .

All night I hide
at the confines of my body,
no defense, no resistance,
one finger to my lips
to keep me from answering.

Back Wards

A fly might influence us,
so we would crawl on our beds,
rub our legs together,
hop backwards, twitch,
touch our bread all over
without eating it.

If a voice in the corridor
said Good Morning
we suffered ecstasy
but if it forecast rain
we panicked: fatal mistake
a moment before healing.

How we feared the visitors!
—huge clammy hands
sometimes not even clean,
palpating as if suffering
had ripened us like fruit.

Did we suffer or they?
When they were gone
we bragged of them:
their size, heft, hue,
the insoluble love
that drove them to Mercy
instead of bridge or tennis:
how they came to look like us—
a crease between the eyes
that was either sorrow
or a hard presentiment:
the gifts they brought us:

grapes, magazines, many Bibles
differing in key passages,
little empty boxes,
wiltless flowers, ribbons,
trophies for enduring,
for never sleeping,
for constant waiting—

while further in the ward
the real patients lie
who have no names,
whom no one visits,
whose cries you might hear
if the gunplay faltered
on the high screens:

they cry without will,
helpless as passing clouds,
just voices, and we,

we would know them
and cry for ourselves.

At Holy Name

The fatigue of the nurse
waiting with the bedpan,
her mind drifting
to a lover's sarcasm;

the unseen child crying;
the panic of the fly
caught in the embrasure
of the window that does not open;

only these are real:
yet I still feel
my mother's hand
cool on my forehead

and her comb untangling
the snarls of a long dream.

The Waiting Room

She said her ex-husband
was a general in the Mexican Army,
a spy, a brain surgeon
who implanted circuits in her mind,

then stalked her, followed her
even down these corridors
that end in a frosted glass door,
an alcove with a slit sofa,

a pie dish full of white ash
and a lucite picture of Saint Jude:
and here she found me
with my name scratched from my bracelet,

I too longing for the lover
who healed me in a past life.

How We Are Made Light

Pity the visitors
bent under shopping bags,
who have kept their huge hats
here where there are no seasons,
who run from station to station
with a question so inconsequential
even we patients smile.

Admire the nurse and the aide
who fill out a form,
one beginning at the front,
the other at the end,
speaking of Bon Jovi;
the doctors, washing side by side,
discussing an even greater doctor;

most of all, revere the orderlies
who have come from across the sea
to wheel us through the corridors
to a place where we will be tested,
where we will finally belong
even more inherently than here,
where we will no longer be watchers
but the matter itself,
flesh and soul transposed
to degrees on a scale of radiance.

Tests

I was put in a machine
shaped like a coffin
and told, wait a minute.

They fastened a strap on my arm
and asked me to think of you,
of home, the child's swing
dangling from the cedar.

Then the strap tightened
and the order came:
imagine sickness in a huge city.

They gave me a mirror
to comb my hair.
It showed an old man.

They weighed me on a scale
that trembled at a breath.

I pissed in a whirling bucket
and coughed in a handkerchief
that was removed instantly
and placed in a sealed container.

They gave me bread and meat
in coded pastel colors,
soft as if already digested.

One seemed to love me
and put needles in my arm,
screwing up his eyes
in anticipated pain.

Another sat on the edge of my bed
and wanted to talk about paradise.

Another had made a map
of the anger in my mind—
a rain of sparks.

They gave me a tiny gown
and no way to close it
except with a child's gesture
of modesty and contrition.

They asked me to count my breaths
and my memories of you.

If a cloud passed
in the high window
I counted it too.

If I saw Venus in darkness
I waited, certain
it would drift down
and become a satellite.

The man from paradise returned
at a late hour with a suitcase
full of identical pictures:

father, mother, and child
walking toward a sun
with little spokes around it.

The light made dreams impossible.

If I dozed, a dazzling lamp
switched on and voices
inquired politely: are you married?

They asked: who is in power?
Who is the enemy?
What great army
is about to attack?

Where will you go
on the day you heal?

The Gift

I cradled that brimming bedpan
and tiptoed as with a sleeping child
toward the toilet at E-13
so the nurse would not comment
on color, odor, and consistency.
Where the stripe in the lino forks
I met you taking your first steps
under orders from the master surgeon
to reach the power doors and return
in under ten minutes—it wouldn't count
unless you actually touched them:
as we passed I felt I was bringing you
a great gift, life
overflowing in its abundance,
though I knew at any moment
the nurse would come running
to wipe away the trail of drops.

Mercy

As I lay waiting for my results
a woman slipped in
humming to herself
a song from the Altiplano.

With a long-necked can
she watered the spider plant
and as she left
she poured a cold jet
in the empty paper cup
on the metal nightstand.

At twilight the doctor came
speaking rapidly, his eyes
flickering from chart to monitor.
I had passed sleep but failed dreams,
passed love but failed hope,
certain high numbers would endure,
    the zeros and fractions would perish.

After he left I waited
for the fronds to droop
so she might come back
singing of Totora
and turn the pot
until the withered leaves
faced where the sun once shone.

Side Effects of Colirium

1

Stifling laughter, but no one to feel it.
We all roll around helpless, doctor, nurse, patient,
like marbles in a bowl—whose joke is this?
The little slice of green grape
suspended in the lime-cherry jello
is killingly funny, and here we are
with our feet in the air
admiring the little pockmarks
in the acoustic tile ceiling—
but they're a riot too!
Pores in Father's nose!
And even the guards
subduing us are giggling,
wrestling us down and yet
waiting, deep within themselves,
for a punch line, any punch line . . .

2

And I in your arms again.

A Night at Mount Sinai

1

The voices return
saying "coleslaw" while I'm eating coleslaw:
what's terrifying about that? Isn't coleslaw
shredded cabbage, or did the voices
just explain that? With a little "mayo"?
Or was it plain mayo?
Surely they are gods without souls.
Did they order: Napkin?
Fork? Knife? Why with a knife
when this substance is nameless
and passes through me
as if I were the Kingdom—
and if I resist
there is no I.

2

I invented this spoon.
And this saltcellar—
someone else made it
and punched the tiny holes,
but I conceived it:
I saw it in a dream
and heard the word: saltcellar:
and no one woke me.

The Parasite

The doctor looked angry
and I too began to choke
with rage at those shadows
who take up all our time
with their uncontrollable desire.

The doctor removed his glasses
and began to clean them
pensively with the hem of his gown.
The room became hazy, intimate.
A file cabinet hovered beside me.
The doctor was a small white cloud.

At once I saw clearly:
it was all my fault.
The bitterness, dizziness
in middle age, a fall,
the beautiful work
suddenly turned incoherent.

The doctor put his fingers together
as if they fitted a special way—
a gesture that would take years to master
and there was so little time,
every second was measured—

and he spoke very softly.
I sensed his great weariness.
I wanted to rock him in my arms.

Rest, he said, night after night
of sleep without terrible dreams.
And work. And loved ones.
Patience, said the doctor, barely audible
above the sweet constant music.

A Prayer for Patience in Sickness

I waited for you as a child
memorizing the signet-ring scratches
on the cut-glass doorknob
until I expected no one
and into the small hours
when I no longer expected to be myself
if the door should open.
    Now you are here
at the other end of my life
and you are the silence in the room,
the light sweeping from wall to wall,
fever itself, no longer just my father.

Saint Anthony's Grounds

I'd like to give the sparrow
a gift—but what? A crumb?

Let it memorize me
and fly over the wall
into the free poplar.

Bright sidelong glance
and a puffed-up strut
as if it were the doctor,
the chief doctor . . .

Soon a flash of wings
and a thread dangling
for a moment in midair . . .

Anoint me in your house
that has no roof or wall—
a patient lost in thought
patting the seam of a white gown
for a ball of lint, a poppy seed,

something small enough, broken enough
to be acceptable in your sight.

Leaving Mary Magdalene

As I was signing out
a guard shuffled up to me
and put his frail hand on my sleeve
asking for discharge papers.
I emptied my pockets.
A snapshot of my child,
sweat-stained, curling inwards.
A Victory dime, a Wheatsheaf penny.
A wisp of thread, a die, a comb.
I looked at him in terror.
He stared back baffled,
angry I had no defense.
A radio was piping in Vivaldi.
I wanted to ask, was it arthritis
that gave him that constant mild tremor
and kept the buttons of his tunic open.
Finally he closed his eyes
and breathed: go,
as if my need were a force like time
and had exhausted him.
I swept up the pennies
and lint from the gleaming counter
afraid to say Thank you
and walked through the winking lights,
the heat shield, the self-opening gates,
into those ice-encrusted streets
where I first learned to be no one.

The author is grateful to the editors of the following magazines: *Areté* (U.K.), "A Night at Mount Sinai," "Treasures of the Cove"; *Columbia: A Journal of Literature and the Arts*, "Honeymoon in Varia"; *Field*, "At Mary Magdalene" (originally published as "At Mount Zion"), "The Dog," "The Engagement" (under the title "Trial Marriage"); *Grand Street*, "At Payless," "Empire Boulevard"; *The Hudson Review*, "Music from an Inner Room" (published under the title "A Delay in Vorkuta"), "The Formal Gardens at Coimbra"; *The Kenyon Review*, "Riding West with Laura," "Northbound," "Cat's-Eye"; *Luna*, "The Part"; *The Manhattan Review*, "The Tower Overlooking the City," "The Book of Splendor," "The Prognosis," "Sunlight," "A Path in Grace"; *The Massachusetts Review*, "Bread and Wine"; *The New Yorker*, "Custody Wars," "Saint Anthony's Grounds," "An Opening in the Largest City"; *The North American Review*, "Back Wards"; *Pivot*, "A Prayer for Patience in Sickness"; *Ploughshares*, "The Play Hour"; *Poetry*, "At Holy Name," "The Waiting Room," "How We Are Made Light," "Tests," "The Gift," "Mercy," "The Parasite," "Leaving Mary Magdalene" (these eight poems published in the suite "Leaving Mary Magdalene"), "Marriage in the Infinite City," "The Rapture," "Riches of the Interior"; *Poetry Ireland Review*, "Leaving Zaragoza," "Black River"; *Poetry Northwest*, "Red-and-Silver Schwinn," "Under the Porch," "The Hellmann's Jar"; *Prairie Schooner*, "Saint Peter's Basement"; *Provincetown Arts*, "Lucky Ford" (published under the title "Arnell Rogers"); *Rattapallax*, "The Migraine"; *TriQuarterly*, "The Threshold"; *The Virginia Quarterly Review*, "The Wilson Avenue Kings"; *Willow Springs*, "Pennies for Flies."

"At Payless" was anthologized in *What Rough Beast: Poems for the End of the Century* (Ashland Poetry Press). "How We Are Made Light" and "Leaving Mary Magdalene" appeared in *Best Poems of 1998* (Roth Electronic Archives). "The Engagement" (under the title "Trial Marriage") appeared in poems.com.

Special thanks to the Artist Fund (New York Foundation for the Arts) for a 2000 grant specific to this book. Thanks also to the National Endowment for the Arts for a fellowship in poetry; to the Mrs. Giles Whiting Foundation; to *Poetry*/The Modern Poetry Foundation for the Bess Hokin Prize, awarded for poems in this manuscript; to the New York Foundation for the Arts; to the Tanne Foundation; and to Yaddo, Blue Mountain Center, the MacDowell Colony, and the Virginia Center for the Creative Arts. With special gratitude to Gerald Freund and to Martha Rhodes.

A NOTE ABOUT THE AUTHOR

D. Nurkse is the author of seven books of poetry. He has
received the Whiting Writers' Award, two National Endow-
ment for the Arts fellowships, two grants from the New York
Foundation for the Arts, a Tanne Foundation award, and the
Bess Hokin Prize from *Poetry*. He has also written widely on
human rights.

A NOTE ON THE TYPE

This book was set in Bodoni, a typeface named after Giam-
battista Bodoni (1740–1813), the celebrated printer and type
designer of Parma. The Bodoni types of today were designed
not as faithful reproductions of any one of the Bodoni fonts but
rather as a composite, modern version of the Bodoni manner.
Bodoni's innovations in type style included a greater degree
of contrast in the thick and thin elements of the letters and
a sharper and more angular finish of details.

Composed by Stratford Publishing Services,
Brattleboro, Vermont
Printed and bound by United Book Press,
Baltimore, Maryland
Designed by Virgina Tan